FREEDOM AT DAWN

Robert Smalls's Voyage Out of Slavery

Leah Schanke

illustrated by
Oboh Moses

Albert Whitman & Company
Chicago, Illinois

Charleston, South Carolina, 1862

My papa, Robert Smalls, is the best boat pilot in Charleston Harbor.

After only a few months as a deckhand, he was promoted to wheelman. Everyone knows that means he's the pilot.

But Mama just shakes her head. "Lizzy, you know that no enslaved man will ever be called a pilot, no matter how good he is at steering a ship."

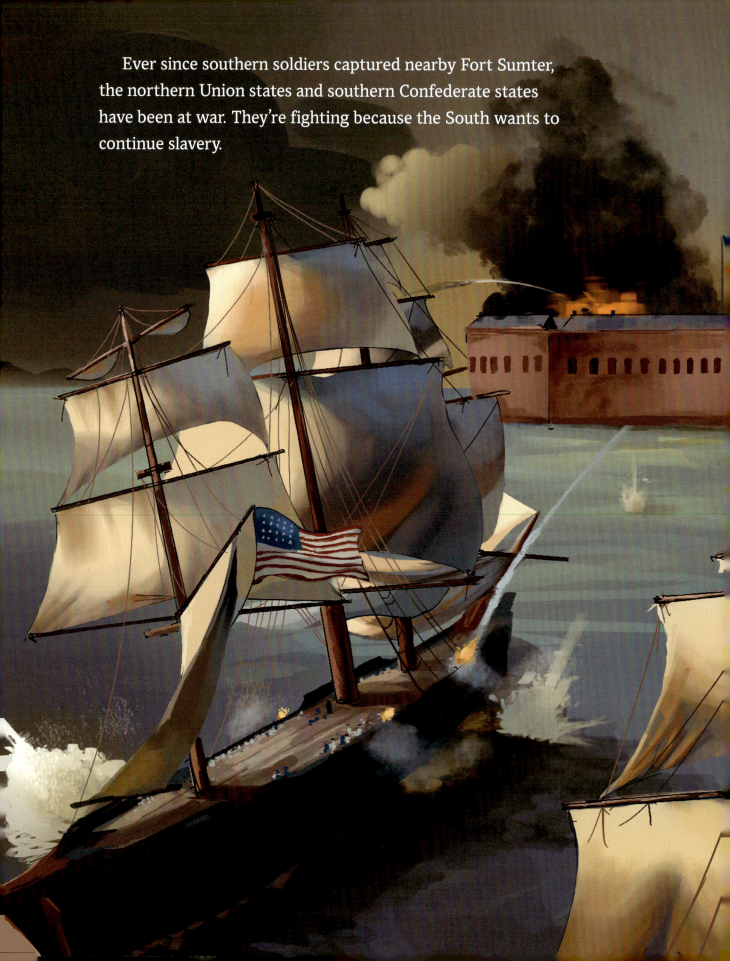

Ever since southern soldiers captured nearby Fort Sumter, the northern Union states and southern Confederate states have been at war. They're fighting because the South wants to continue slavery.

Because they are enslaved, Papa and his shipmates on the *Planter* have no choice but to help the South in the war. Even worse, Papa could still come home any night and find Mama, Baby Robert, and me gone forever because our owner sold us.

Mama and Papa agree: now is the time to escape to freedom by taking over the *Planter* and steering it out to the Union ships in the Atlantic Ocean nearby. But no one can pass Fort Sumter and leave the harbor unless they signal with the secret sequence of long and short blows of the ship's whistle.

Papa knows the secret whistle code. Dressed as the captain, he could sail in the dark of night past the forts and guard crews with their big guns. But if we were captured trying to escape, the men on the ship would be killed. The women and children would be sold to different owners. Families would be separated.

Mama says to Papa, "It's a risk, but we must be free. Where you go, our family will go. If you die, we all die."

Papa's six shipmates agree to keep the plan a secret.

We wait until Papa says it's time to put his plan into action. After a couple of weeks, he tells us that the Confederate general is expecting the North to attack Charleston. The harbor will soon be even more heavily guarded than usual. Tonight could be our last chance to escape.

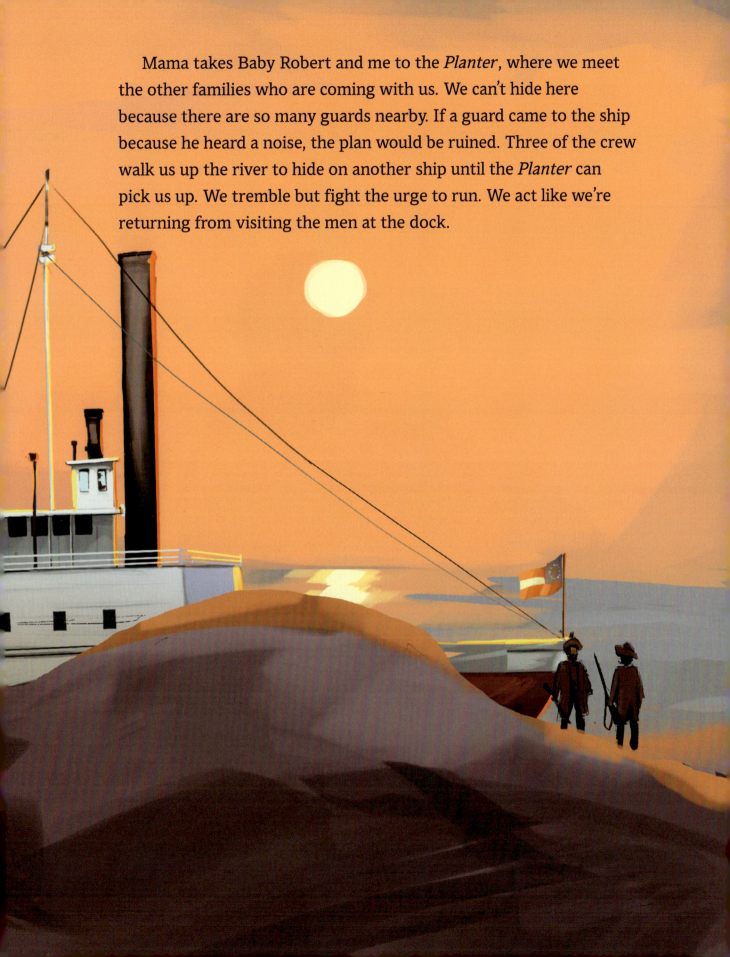

Mama takes Baby Robert and me to the *Planter*, where we meet the other families who are coming with us. We can't hide here because there are so many guards nearby. If a guard came to the ship because he heard a noise, the plan would be ruined. Three of the crew walk us up the river to hide on another ship until the *Planter* can pick us up. We tremble but fight the urge to run. We act like we're returning from visiting the men at the dock.

One hour passes, and then another. Is Papa coming? The men pace back and forth. If we leave the ship, we could be caught without a pass to be on the street late at night. We would all be arrested. We can only wait and worry.

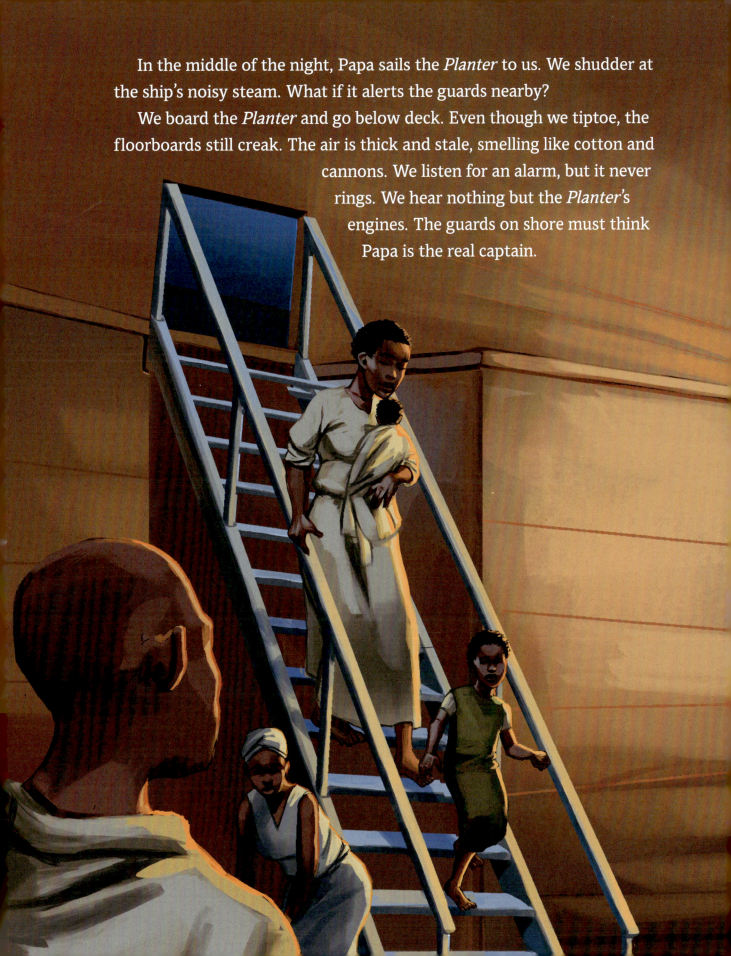

In the middle of the night, Papa sails the *Planter* to us. We shudder at the ship's noisy steam. What if it alerts the guards nearby?

We board the *Planter* and go below deck. Even though we tiptoe, the floorboards still creak. The air is thick and stale, smelling like cotton and cannons. We listen for an alarm, but it never rings. We hear nothing but the *Planter*'s engines. The guards on shore must think Papa is the real captain.

WHOO! WHOO!

Someone's pulled the *Planter*'s whistle cord.
"Mama, are we leaving the harbor already?"
"No, it's too soon. Your papa must be giving a friendly salute to a guard boat."

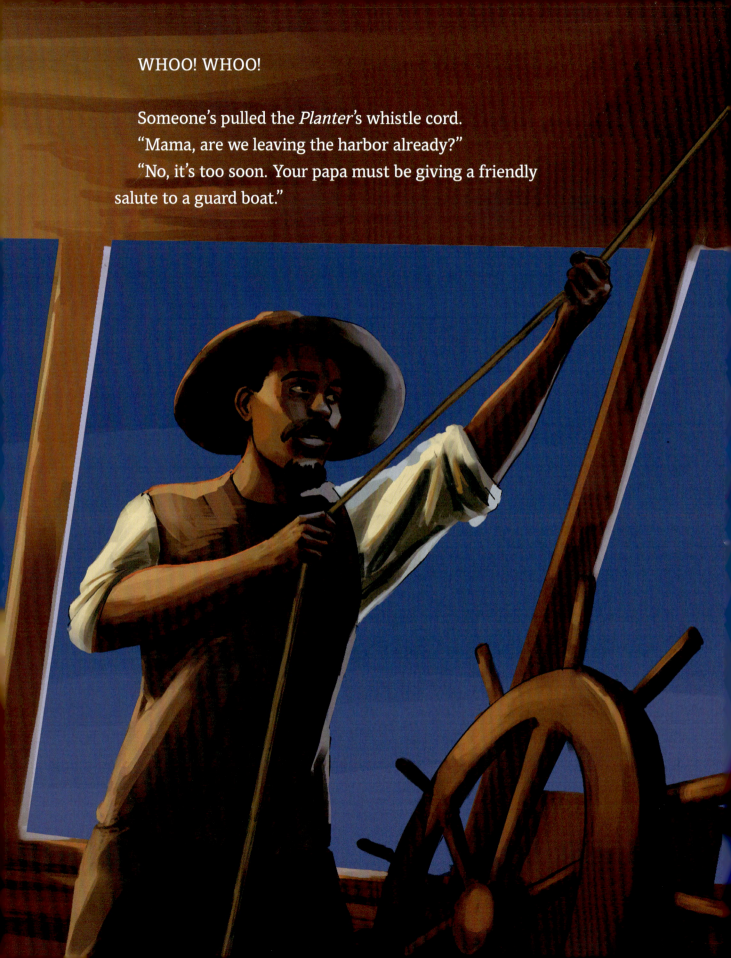

Papa and his crew sail slow and steady past more boats and forts. Speeding would give us away.

"Mama, it's almost morning. When it gets light the men at the next fort might see that Papa's skin isn't white."

Mama strokes my arm. "I know, Lizzy. But if we can make it out of the harbor before the sun comes up, we'll find freedom at dawn."

I try to be brave like Mama and Papa. I keep my head up.
I don't cry. I sit on my shaking hands to keep them still. The
women are crying quietly or praying in whispers.

WHOOOOO! WHOOOOO! WHOO!
Papa blows the secret whistle code. We're finally passing Fort Sumter. We all hold our breath.

The *Planter* speeds up as she heads out to sea toward the Union ships. I hear men's voices. Are they Union soldiers? I run up to the deck to see.

"No, Lizzy, wait!" Mama shouts.

But the voices I heard weren't Union soldiers at all. They were the Confederate soldiers at Fort Sumter.

They yell and signal to the guards across the harbor. "Fire! Fire!"

I thought we were safely past the fort. But they spotted us.

I squat and cover my ears. I wait for the *Planter* to be hit.
"Be free or die. I will be free or die...."

But the shots never come. The *Planter* is too far away for the guns at the fort to hit it.

CLANG! CLANG! CLANG!

Just then, the closest Union ship sounds an alarm. We're not out of trouble yet! We escaped the harbor into the sea, but we look like an enemy to the Union ships. One of the ships turns to point its guns at us. Papa's shipmates are shaking as much as I am. But not Papa.

Our crew rushes to raise a white sheet. It's a sign that we won't fire on the Union ships. But will they see it in time? The darkness that hid us during our voyage out of the harbor works against us now.

"Hold your fire!" I hear the Union ship's captain shout to his men.

The Union ship pulls alongside the *Planter*. Papa scoops me up into his arms.

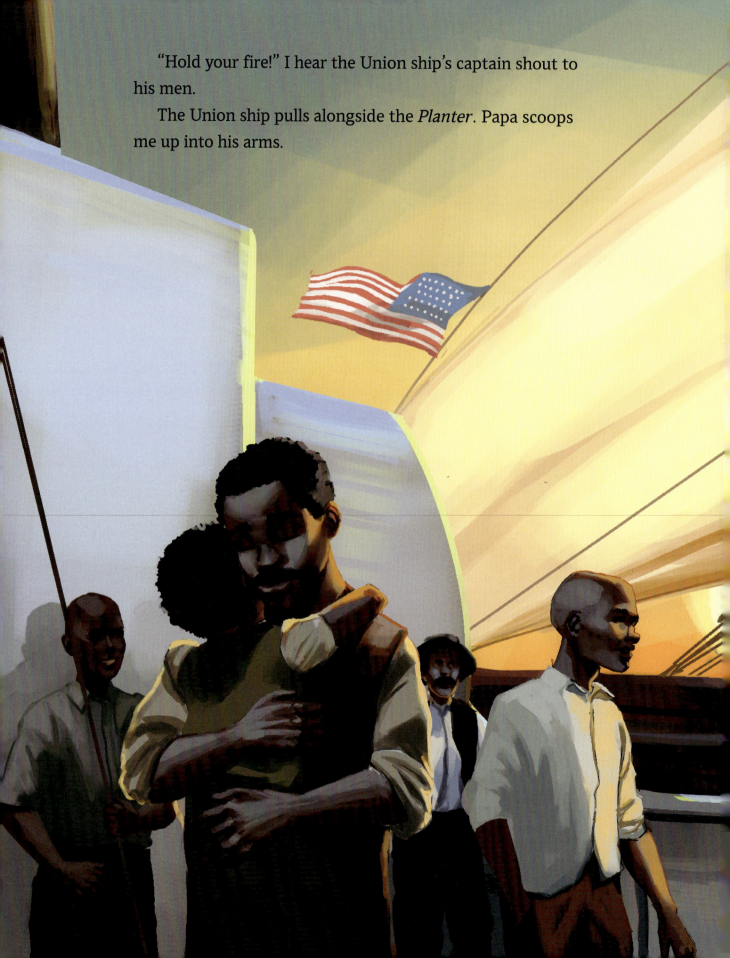

The Union captain doesn't see one white person aboard the *Planter*. "You piloted this ship through that harbor without being fired upon?" he asks, his face showing his surprise.

"Yes, sir. Good morning, sir," Papa says. "And I've brought you the Confederate guns that were packed below deck."

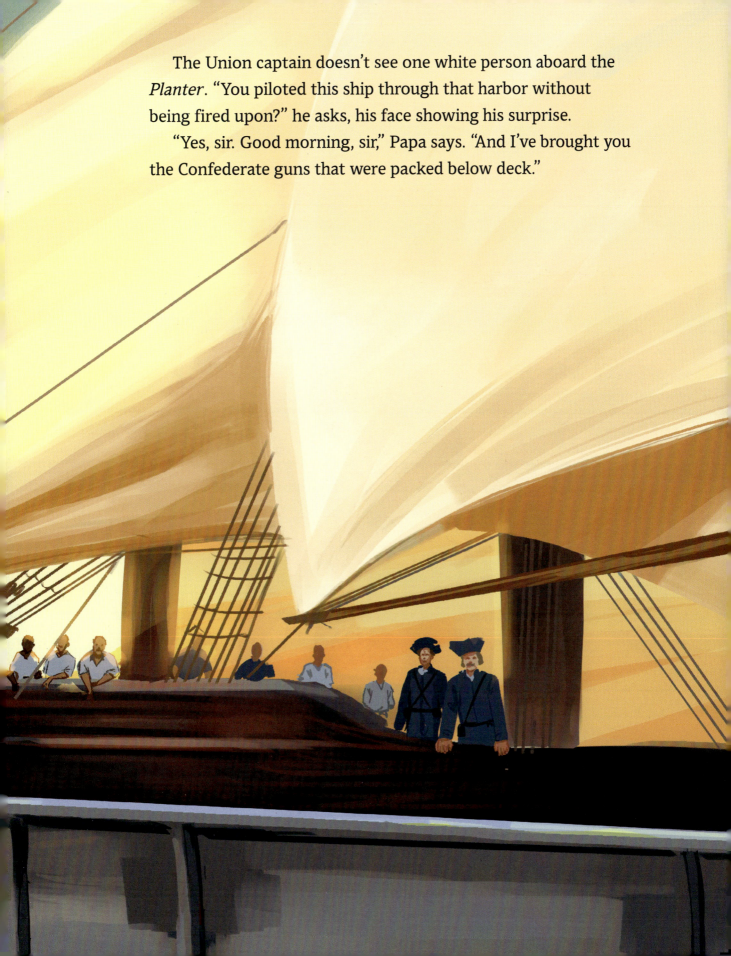

With Baby Robert in her arms, Mama rushes up from below deck. Everyone else follows, jumping up and down and dancing.

They cry out, "Freedom at dawn! Freedom at dawn!"

"We're free! We're free!"

I hug Papa as hard as I can. I always knew he was the best boat pilot in the harbor. And now he's proven it to everyone by fearlessly steering us out of slavery.

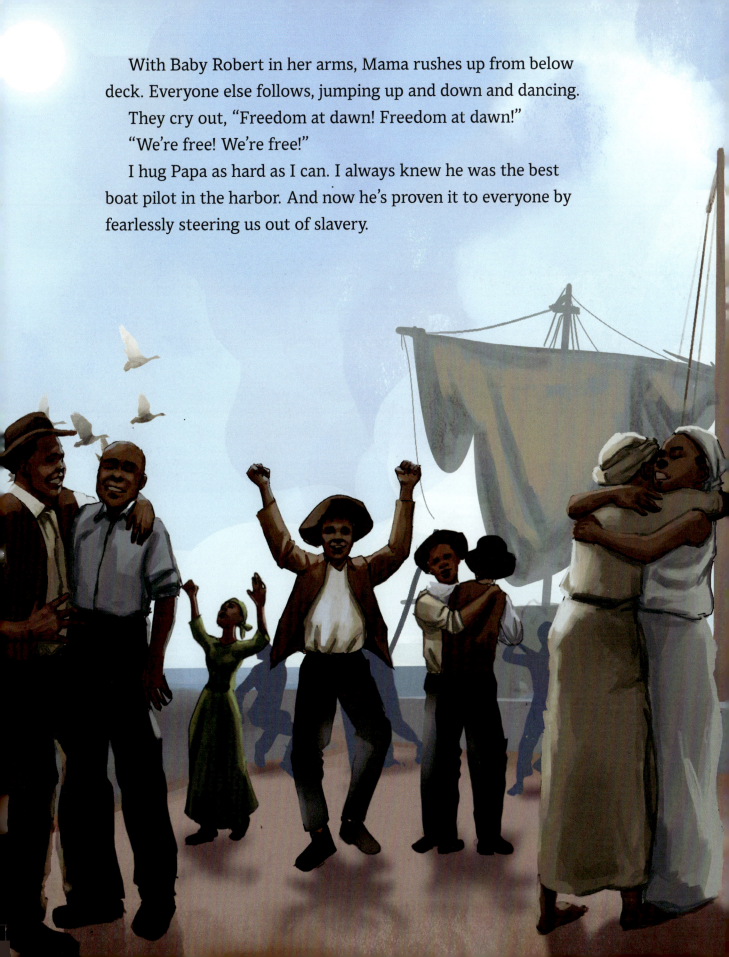

For the first time, I look out at the horizon as a free person. I squeeze Papa's hand, dreaming of a time when there will be freedom for all.

The US Civil War

The US Civil War was the result of a division between northern states and southern states over whether slavery would be allowed in newly forming states in the western part of the country.

By the early 1800s, there were nearly four million enslaved people in the South. They were forced to do backbreaking work to grow cotton, sugar, and other valuable crops. People in the southern states feared that newly created western states would be barred from allowing slavery. States allowing slavery would then be heavily outnumbered in Congress. This would make a national ban against slavery very likely.

In December 1860, one month after Abraham Lincoln—who opposed allowing slavery in the West—was elected president, South Carolina became the first state to secede from, or leave, the United States. A total of eleven southern states eventually seceded to form the Confederate States of America, or the Confederacy. On April 12, 1861, the Confederate army captured Fort Sumter from the US military. This began a four-year civil war between the Confederacy and the remaining US states in the North, called the Union. The nation was torn in two. Hundreds of thousands of people were killed before the Confederate armies surrendered in spring of 1865. In December 1865, slavery was officially ended in all states.

Author's Note

Robert Smalls's daring escape on May 13, 1862, during the US Civil War, became headline news in the North. Smalls's wife, Hannah Jones, and their two children, Elizabeth Lydia (Lizzy) and Robert, Jr., escaped with him, along with twelve others. Though this story is told from Lizzy's point of view, historical facts indicate that she remained below deck through the entire escape.

After the escape, the Union hired Smalls to continue piloting the *Planter*—this time against the Confederacy. Smalls fought in seventeen battles, helping the Union to win the war.

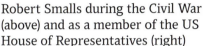

Robert Smalls during the Civil War (above) and as a member of the US House of Representatives (right)

After the war, Smalls purchased the house where he was born in Beaufort, South Carolina. With a strong belief in the power of education, he sent his children to the best schools in the United States. Smalls himself learned to read and write in his twenties and served five terms in the US House of Representatives. Lizzy worked as a secretary at a school for newly freed African Americans in the Sea Islands near South Carolina. She married and had eleven children before dying in 1959 at the age of 101 in Charlotte, North Carolina.

Today, Smalls is remembered as a hero of the Civil War. The Robert Smalls House in Beaufort, South Carolina, was designated a National Historic Landmark in 1974. And on September 15, 2007, many of Robert Smalls's descendants attended the US Army's commission of a new ship named USAV *Major General Robert Smalls* in Baltimore, Maryland. It was the first Army ship named after an African American.

USAV *Major General Robert Smalls*

For my family, especially A.E.S. and E.B.S., where this journey began.—LS

To those without fast legs nor smoothness of tongue, to the fainthearted, may this book ignite your imagination and illuminate your path.—OM

Library of Congress Cataloging-in-Publication data is on file with the publisher.
Text copyright © 2025 by Leah Schanke
Illustrations copyright © 2025 by Albert Whitman & Company
Illustrations by Oboh Moses
First published in the United States of America in 2025 by Albert Whitman & Company
ISBN 978-0-8075-2428-2 (hardcover)
ISBN 978-0-8075-2429-9 (ebook)
All rights reserved. No part of this book may be reproduced or transmitted in any form or by any means, electronic or mechanical, including photocopying, recording, or by any information storage and retrieval system, without permission in writing from the publisher.

Page 31 photo credits:
Left: Robert Smalls (1839-1915), Pilot of the 'Planter',
Samuel Francis du Pont photographs, 2010_269_W9_18823, Hagley Museum and Library;
Right: Library of Congress

Printed in Canada
10 9 8 7 6 5 4 3 2 1 TCP 30 29 28 27 26 25

Design by Rick DeMonico

For more information about Albert Whitman & Company,
visit our website at www.albertwhitman.com